Kids Are Cookin'

Kid-tested, mom-approved, crowd-pleasing, amazingly awesome, delightfully delicious, terrifically tasty, especially scrumptious, tried-and-true, blue-ribbon, award-winning,

ALL-TIME-FAVORITE RECIPES THAT KIDS LOVE TO COOK!

by Karen Brown

 **Meadowbrook Press**

Distributed by Simon & Schuster
New York

Library of Congress Cataloging-in-Publication Data

Brown, Karen, 1952 Feb. 19-
    Kids are cookin' / by Karen Brown.
        p. cm.
    Includes index.
    Summary: Recipes for all sorts of foods that kids like and can fix themselves or with minimal help
from parents.
    ISBN 0-88166-279-8. — ISNBN 0-671-57552-X (Simon & Schuster)
    1. Cookery—Juvenile literature. [1. Cookery.] I. Title.
TX652.5.B743 1997
641.5'123—dc21   96-29926
                                                                                CIP
                                                                                 AC

Editor: Liya Lev Oertel
Copyeditor: Victoria Hall
Production Manager: Amy Unger
Production Assistant: Danielle White
Text Illustrations: Laurel Aiello
Cover Illustration: Gwen Connelly

Published by Meadowbrook Press, 5451 Smetana Drive, Minnetonka, MN 55343

BOOK TRADE DISTRIBUTION by Simon & Schuster, a division of Simon and Schuster, Inc., 1230
Avenue of the Americas, New York, NY 10020

00 99 98 97   4 3 2 1

Printed in the United States of America

For my son Barrett,
who provides inspiration ...
and a willing appetite.

CONTENTS

A Note to Parents of Young Chefs

Remember helping your mom in the kitchen—how much fun it was to grate cheese, stir cookie dough, and, especially, to lick the spoon? You can recreate those fond memories and start new traditions for your children with these simple recipes designed especially for their appetites.

The step-by-step instructions are quick and easy, and require just a little help from you, depending on your child's age. No matter what your child's age or cooking ability, take the opportunity to review safety rules with your junior cooks:

1. Always ask for an adult's help when using knives or kitchen equipment such as mixers and blenders.
2. Turn pot and pan handles to the inside, so hot food can't be knocked off the stovetop.
3. Take care when removing dishes from hot ovens. Always use thick, insulated potholders or mitts.
4. When baking, make sure that the baking dishes are Pyrex, metal, or other oven-proof material.
5. When using the microwave, make sure the dishes are microwave safe— never metal.
6. If using a nonstick pan, use plastic or wooden utencils (spatulas, spoons, etc.) to avoid scratching the nonstick surface.
7. When preheating a pan or skillet, don't forget it. Preheating should never take longer than 5 minutes. A hot skillet could cause burns.
8. When preheating the oven, make sure not to forget about it. Remove everything but the oven racks from the oven before turning it on.

Family participation in menu planning, grocery shopping, and food preparation can be a real adventure for everyone. And this participation often helps relieve doubts about new foods for the picky eaters in your house. Let the little ones help measure and stir, while older cooks can wash greens and chop vegetables. You will end up with a houseful of enthusiastic gourmets and, hopefully, a new generation of experienced kitchen assistants!

For rainy days, special occasions, or when you just feel like being creative— we've assembled an array of family favorites that we hope you'll enjoy. My best wishes to you and your children for many warm and wonderful times in the kitchen, with food that's both fun to make and fun to eat!

Happy Cooking!

Karen Brown

WET YOUR WHISTLE

Warm-You-Up Hot Cocoa

Sleeping in a tent in the back yard. Got your canteen and compass. Sleeping bag is pretty comfortable. Then your big brother starts telling ghost stories. Things start to seem scary, and you decide to move inside. To warm up (and put a lid on those goose bumps), you make hot cocoa. Not the instant stuff—but real milk and real chocolate. Because you're a one-hundred-percent genuine person who likes honest food. Mmmmmm!

Makes 4 steaming mugs of cocoa.

Ingredients

⅓ cup cocoa
⅓ cup sugar
¼ teaspoon salt
½ cup water
3½ cups milk

Materials

Large saucepan
Large spoon (for stirring)
4 mugs

1 In a saucepan over medium-high heat, stir together first 4 ingredients and bring to a boil.

2 Reduce heat and add milk, stirring until hot.

3 Turn off the heat and pour into mugs.

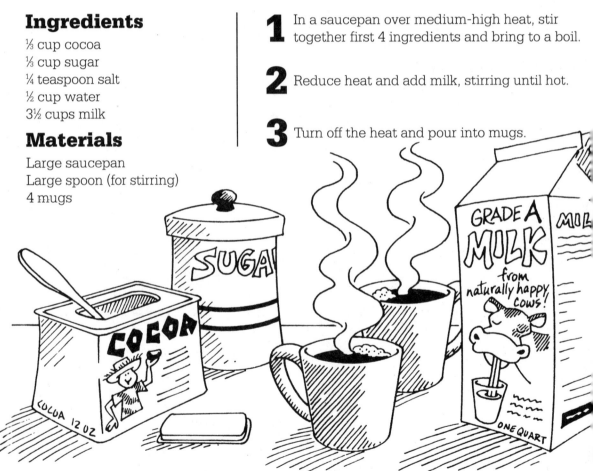

Tip: Try not to let the milk boil. If it does and a skin forms on the top, just skim it off with a spoon. (Unless you like the skin. Then slurp it down!)

Smells-So-Good Cinnamon Apple Cider

Sweet dreams.
Sleep tight.
Don't let the bedbugs bite.
Snuggle down with your favorite blanket and a steaming mug of cider, for the coziest bedtime ever.

Makes about 4 cups.

Ingredients

1 quart sweet apple cider
2 cinnamon sticks
1 teaspoon ground cloves
½ teaspoon nutmeg

Materials

Large saucepan
Wooden spoon (for stirring)
Strainer
4 cups or mugs

1 In large saucepan, stir spices into cider and simmer for about 10 minutes over moderate heat.

2 Pour through a strainer with small holes to remove the spices that haven't dissolved.

3 Serve piping hot.

Tip: When straining the cider, make sure that the holes in the strainer are smaller than the spices you are trying to catch.

Best-Ever Banana-and-Berry Smoothies

Mt. Kilimanjaro.
Mt. Everest.
The highest monkey bar.
Whatever your journey, whatever your goal, you'll need a healthy drink first!

Makes 2 smoothies.

Ingredients

1 cup milk
1 banana
1 cup blueberries or straw
   berries, fresh or frozen
1 cup fruit-flavored yogurt

Materials

Blender
2 glasses

1 In a blender, combine milk and fruit, blending until smooth.

2 Add yogurt and blend at low speed for 1 or 2 minutes.

Tip: You will know when the smoothie is ready when all the ingredients are completely blended together.

Fuzzy Purple Cow

You're sitting on the front porch, watching your dog chase fireflies, and Joey DePalma is making fun of your purple teeth. But you don't care, because this grape drink is your favorite, and you just might not let him have any (if he's going to be that way).

Makes 1 glass.

Ingredients

1 pint lemon or lime sherbet
1 24-ounce bottle purple
  grape juice
1 16-ounce club soda or
  ginger ale

Materials

1 tall glass
Ice cream scoop (or large
  spoon)
Long spoon (for stirring)

1 Put 1 to 2 scoops of sherbet in a tall glass.

2 Pour grape juice on top of the sherbet until the glass is about ⅔ full.

3 Top off with club soda and stir until you have the shade of purple that you like.

Tip: You will have leftovers of everything, so make more and share.

Real Lemonade

School's out. Summer's here. It's hot enough to fry an egg on the sidewalk. Today's just the day to make some big bucks from a lemonade stand with old-fashioned, honest-to-goodness, not-from-a-mix real lemonade.

Makes 2 glasses of lemonade.

Ingredients

3 lemons
¼ to ½ cup sugar
2 cups water
1 cup ice

Materials

Knife
Cutting board
Medium bowl
Strainer
Pitcher
Long spoon (for stirring)
2 tall glasses

1 Slice lemons on a cutting board and squeeze each lemon slice into a bowl.

2 To remove seeds, pour the squeezed lemon juice through strainer into pitcher.

3 Add sugar and water, mixing well. Pour into glasses filled with ice.

Tip: If you want your lemonade to be more tart, add less sugar, and then try not to giggle at the faces your customers will make!

Special Sparkly Orange Fizz

Simon Says. Mother, May I?
Swinging Statues.
Duck, Duck, Goose.
Red Rover, Red Rover.
Whew! All that hard work can really make a kid thirsty!

Makes 3 glasses.

Ingredients

2 glasses orange juice
1 glass club soda, seltzer, or
   other sparkling, flavorless
   soda
3 orange slices

Materials

3 glasses

1 For each serving, fill glass about ⅔ full of orange juice and add club soda to the top.

2 Garnish glass with orange slice.

Tip: This drink works well with many juices, such as pineapple or grape, and you can add a maraschino cherry on top instead of the orange slice!

Just-Like-the-Malt-Shop's Chocolate Milk Shake

He cruises into the malt shop. Leather jacket. Slicked-back hair. So cool. He orders a chocolate shake. Everyone stops to stare, but not you. You grab a straw and, with a confident smile, ask him if you can share. As you sip the shake together, he gazes deep into your eyes...

Then you wake up from your dream. Oh, well. Is there any ice cream in the freezer?

Makes 1 large shake.

Ingredients

2 scoops chocolate ice cream
1 cup milk
2 teaspoons chocolate syrup

Materials

Blender
Ice cream scoop (or large
    spoon)
1 tall glass

1 Put all ingredients into blender and whip for 30 seconds, or until frothy.

2 Pour into a tall glass and enjoy.

Tip: Experiment! To create a variety of taste treats, use butterscotch syrup, chopped strawberries, creamy peanut butter, and other tasty treats instead of the chocolate syrup!

Sweet-'N'-Dreamy Root Beer Float

Down the hatch.
Bottoms up.
Chug-a-lug.
You'll want to get to the bottom of this, because it's so-o-o good.

Makes 1 tall glass.

Ingredients

2 scoops vanilla ice cream
1 glass root beer

Materials

Ice cream scoop (or large
    spoon)
1 tall glass
Straws
Long spoon

1 Place ice cream in tall glass, and fill to top with root beer.

2 Serve with straws and a long spoon.

Tip: Pour the root beer slowly, so you don't get a lot of foam.

Shake-It-Up-Baby Peach Cooler

Rock and roll!
Twist and shout!
Move and groove!

Makes 1 glass.

Ingredients

1 cup milk
1 cup peach slices, fresh or
  frozen
1 teaspoon sugar
½ teaspoon vanilla
3 ice cubes

Materials

Blender
1 tall glass

1 Place first 4 ingredients in blender and mix
together.

2 Add ice cubes and blend until smooth. Pour
into a tall glass.

Tip: If the peaches are frozen and still have some ice on them, you may not need to add
all 3 ice cubes. After doing Step 1, taste the shake to see if it needs all the ice.

WAKER-UPPERS

Fluffy French Cinnamon Toast

Your first slumber party. You painted toenails, called 7 boys, and tried on everyone's clothes. (And that was just the first hour!) But the best part was making your own French toast for breakfast. Everyone cleaned their plates.

Makes 3 serving (2 slices per person).

Ingredients

6 slices bread
3 eggs
¼ cup milk
1 tablespoon cold water
1 tablespoon cinnamon
2 tablespoons margarine

Materials

Whisk or fork
Medium bowl
Skillet
Spatula
3 plates

1 In a bowl, beat together eggs, milk, water, and cinnamon with a wisk or fork.

2 Gently pierce bread slices with fork and soak both sides in egg mixture.

3 Heat margarine in skillet on medium heat. Add bread slices, cooking and turning until golden on each side.

4 Transfer to plates and top with your favorite syrup or jam.

Tip: After Step 1, pour the egg mixture into a wide, shallow bowl. Dipping the bread will be easier this way.

Come-and-Get-It Blueberry Pancakes

Blueberry pancakes are perfect for those Saturday mornings when you're just hanging out, wearing your bunny slippers, and watching cartoons. It just doesn't get any better than this!

Makes 6 to 8 pancakes.

Ingredients

1 egg
2 tablespoons vegetable oil
¾ cup milk
1 cup flour
1 tablespoon sugar
2 teaspoons baking powder
½ teaspoon salt
½ cup blueberries

Materials

2 mixing bowls
Fork, tablespoon
Spatula
Griddle or skillet
Plates

1 In mixing bowl, beat egg with fork; then add oil and milk and beat again.

2 In a separate bowl, mix together flour, sugar, baking powder, and salt; then combine with egg mixture.

3 Carefully fold in blueberries, mixing gently to avoid making blueberry mush.

4 Pour a little oil onto the griddle or skillet and move the griddle from side to side to spread the oil. Then pour a large tablespoon of batter onto hot, greased griddle or skillet.

5 When bubbles form on top of pancakes, flip them carefully with a spatula, and continue cooking until both sides are golden brown.

6 Pile pancakes onto plates and serve with your favorite syrup or jam topping.

Tip: You can also invent your own pancakes: Use chocolate chips instead of blueberries; add drops of food coloring to the batter and make pink pancakes, blue pancakes, or your favorite color; use cookie cutters for fun shapes—use alphabet cutters for your initials!

Energizing Eggs with a Hat

It's the first day of school, and you want to make a good impression. You've got the most politically correct backpack, the most environmentally safe school supplies, and now you need the best breakfast ever.

Serves 1 person.

Ingredients

1 tablespoon margarine
1 slice bread
1 egg
Salt and pepper, to taste

Materials

Small juice glass or cookie
    cutter
Skillet
Spatula
Toaster
Plate

1 Using a small juice glass or cookie cutter, cut a hole out of the middle of the bread slice. Save the round piece to use later.

2 Melt margarine in skillet over medium heat, and place bread slice in pan.

3 Gently crack an egg into the hole of the bread slice and cook until set. Using a spatula, flip the egg and bread together and cook for another minute, until egg is done.

4 Put the round piece of bread (the one you have put aside in Step 1) in the toaster and toast lightly.

5 Serve cooked egg-toast on a plate with its round "hat" on top.

6 Sprinkle with salt and pepper as desired.

Tips: When you melt the margarine in Step 2, don't let it sit in the pan too long without adding the toast. Burnt margarine smells funny. Also, keep in mind that the melted margarine is HOT and may splatter. So be very careful.

Rise 'N' Shine Breakfast Pockets

Important trip to the mall today. You need athletic shoes. Decisions, decisions.
Flashing lights in the heels?
Air pump?
Laces should be cool, yet not too trendy.
What, we have to eat breakfast first? Okay, but let's make it snappy.

Makes 2 pockets.

Ingredients

4 eggs
4 tablespoons cold water
1 tablespoon margarine
¼ cup cheese, grated
Salt and pepper, to taste
1 pita-bread round

Materials

Large bowl
Skillet
Fork, knife, tablespoon

1 In a bowl, beat together eggs and cold water with a fork.

2 Melt margarine in skillet and add egg mixture.

3 Cook and stir on low to medium heat for a few minutes. Add grated cheese, salt, and pepper, scrambling for another 5 minutes, or until eggs are cooked.

4 Cut the pita round in half and open each half to make pockets. Spoon scrambled eggs into each pocket.

Tips: If you do not have a grater at home, you can buy many cheeses already grated: mozzarella, Cheddar, and so on. Also, you can add bacon bits or salsa for a more flavorful waker-upper.

Good-Morning Cheese Omelets

Good morning to you,
Good morning to you.
We're all in our places,
With egg on our faces.

Makes 1 omelet.

Ingredients

Nonstick cooking spray
2 eggs
1 tablespoon cold water
¼ cup cheese, grated
Salt and pepper, to taste

Materials

Skillet
Fork
Spatula
Plate

1 Coat skillet with nonstick cooking spray and heat over low setting until hot. (You can test whether the skillet is hot by dropping a drop of water onto it—if the water sizzles and disappears, the skillet is hot. Be sure not to let the skillet heat too long or it will burn.)

2 With a fork, beat together eggs and water until frothy and pour into hot skillet.

3 Sprinkle with salt and pepper, and carefully tilt pan to let egg mixture cook evenly.

4 Sprinkle grated cheese on top (see grated cheese tip on page 15), and continue cooking until cheese is melted and egg is done. (Should be lightly browned on bottom and firm on top.)

5 Gently lift sides with spatula, fold in half, and slide onto plate.

Tips: While the omelet is cooking, cover it with a lid. This way the heat will be distributed throughout the omelet and cook inside as well as outside. Also, be creative and make different kinds of omelets—add bacon bits, ham slices, chopped onion, chopped green pepper, or chopped mushrooms. Just add any (or all!) of those ingredients to the omelet together with the cheese.

Baked Breakfast Cheese Puffs

Did the alarm go off?
It's too early!
Let me sleep for just five more minutes!
Even the laziest of sleepyheads will bound out of bed for this delicious concoction!

Makes 4 puffs.

Ingredients

8 slices sandwich bread
4 slices American cheese
2 eggs, slightly beaten
2 cups milk
½ teaspoon salt
2 tablespoons margarine

Materials

8-inch square baking dish
Knife
Medium bowl
4 plates

1 Take an 8-inch square baking dish (make sure that it is oven-proof) and coat its inside sides and bottom with a thin layer of margarine or butter.

2 Trim crusts from bread and place 4 slices of the 8 bread slices into the greased baking pan.

3 Layer cheese slices on top, then add remaining layer of bread.

4 In a separate bowl, mix together eggs, milk, and salt; then pour over bread layers.

5 Dot with margarine and bake at 350 degrees for 45 to 60 minutes, or until golden and puffy.

6 Cool slightly and slice into squares.

Tips: Greasing the pan prevents the food from burning or sticking to the baking dish. If you are using stick margarine or butter, you can grease the pan easily by unwrapping one end of the stick and, while holding the other, wrapped, end with your hand, draw on the pan with the margarine! Another easy greasing method is to put a bit of margarine or butter onto a paper towel and spread a thin layer over the pan.

Just-Right Oatmeal

The first winter storm, and you're going to make a snowman!
What do you need?
A carrot for his nose and pipe for his mouth.
Boots and mittens for you.
And to keep you warm, a just-right breakfast.

Makes 2 servings.

Ingredients

1½ cups water
½ teaspoon salt
1 teaspoon butter or
    margarine
⅔ cup quick-cooking oatmeal
    (such as Quaker Quick Oats®)
½ cup raisins
2 tablespoons brown sugar
Milk or cream, to taste

Materials

Large saucepan
Wooden spoon (for stirring)
Tablespoon
2 serving bowls

1 Bring water to a boil in large saucepan, then add salt, butter or margarine, oatmeal, and raisins.

2 Stir over medium-to-low heat for about 1 minute, or until creamy.

3 Remove from heat, cover, and let sit for a few minutes.

4 Top with brown sugar and milk.

Tip: Applesauce is also an extra-delicious topping for oatmeal.

Fabulous Fresh Fruit K-Bobs

Down at the Farmer's Market, truck beds are filled with every kind of fruit you've ever seen, and some you've never seen. Which do you like: strawberries? watermelon? pineapple? kiwi? Can't decide? Which colors look good together?

Each skewer makes 1 serving.

Ingredients

1 cup pineapple chunks
1 cup strawberry pieces
1 cup seedless grapes
1 cup melon chunks

Materials

Wooden skewers

1 Carefully slide fruit pieces onto skewers, alternating one fruit at a time.

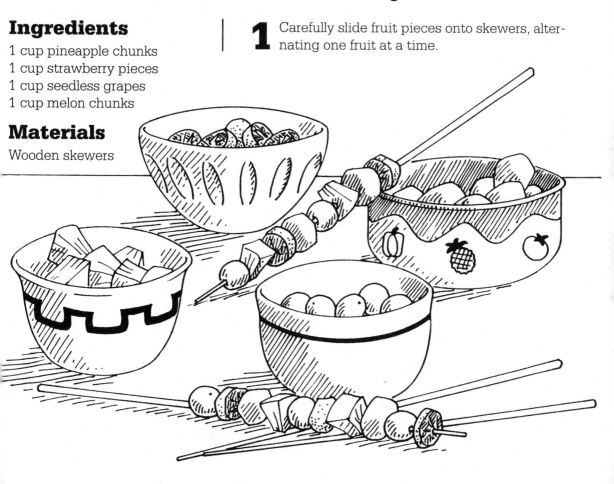

Tip: By adding sandwich meat and cubes of cheese, you can turn these k-bobs into lunch!

Scrumptiously Sweet Baked Apples

You stretch and decide to stay in bed for another few minutes. But what's that smell? Could it be baked apples? Umm, good. Your dad likes his apples hot from the oven, with sour cream on top. You like yours plain, and cooled a little. But you'd better jump out of bed and get down to the kitchen before they're all gone!

Makes 4 baked apples.

Ingredients

4 small to medium apples
4 teaspoons margarine
4 teaspoons brown sugar
4 tablespoons raisins
Cinnamon

Materials

Apple corer
Knife, spoon
Baking dish
Aluminum foil

1 Wash the apples and slice a little off the tops. Then take the cores out using a special apple corer or a knife. Place cored apples in a baking dish.

2 Fill center of each apple with 1 teaspoon margarine, 1 teaspoon brown sugar, and 1 tablespoon raisins.

3 Sprinkle a dash of cinnamon on top of each apple.

4 Fill the baking dish with half an inch of water and cover with aluminum foil.

5 Bake at 375 degrees for 1 hour, or until tender.

Tip: When you are coring the apples, leave the bottom of the apple intact, or all the stuff you'll put into it will fall out once you pick the apple up.

Hip-Hip-Hooray Hash Browns

One potato, two potato,
three potato, four.
When you taste these hash browns,
you'll want more!

Makes 4 servings.

Ingredients

3 medium potatoes, peeled
   and diced into very small
   cubes
1 teaspoon lemon juice
¼ cup onion, grated
1 tablespoon parsley
3 tablespoons oil
Salt and pepper, to taste

Materials

Large mixing bowl
Large skillet
Fork
Spatula or wooden spoon
   (for stirring)

1 In large mixing bowl, sprinkle lemon juice over potatoes; then stir in grated onion and parsley.

2 In large skillet, heat oil over medium heat, and pour in potato mixture. Cook and turn until all sides are browned and potatoes are soft and easily cut with a fork.

3 Sprinkle with salt and pepper and serve warm.

Tip: Instead of cutting the potatoes into cubes, grate them using the side of the grater
   with the biggest holes (so you don't make potato sauce!).

BOUNTIFUL BREADS
and
MARVELOUS MUFFINS

Piping Hot Puffed-Up Popovers

"Less is more." It doesn't make much sense, but in this case, it's true. These simple popovers are so quick and easy to make, that you won't believe how delicious they taste! And they're so simple to serve with just butter or jam. But if you've got a sweet tooth, you can also turn them into a dessert dish, dusted with confectioner's sugar and filled with your favorite custard or pudding. In which case, "more is mine."

Makes 12 large rolls.

Ingredients

3 eggs
1½ cups milk
2 tablespoons butter, melted
1½ cups flour
½ teaspoon salt

Materials

Electric mixer
Large bowl
Medium bowl
Muffin tins

1 In a large bowl, beat together eggs, milk, and butter using electric mixer, until frothy.

2 Mix together flour and salt in a separate bowl; then add to egg mixture, blending well.

3 Pour into generously buttered muffin tins (see greasing tip on page 17) and bake at 450 degrees for 15 minutes; then reduce temperature to 350 degrees and continue baking for 20 more minutes.

4 Pop out of the tins and serve immediately.

Tip: Be sure to mix the flour and salt well, so you don't get all the salt in one bite. Yuk!

Delectably Delicious Drop Biscuits

Going to your cousin's place to try on his hand-me-downs. (And you know there's gonna be some goofy-looking stuff there. There always is.) Hmm…that cool ski jacket of his fits you perfectly. Then you stay for supper and get to help with the biscuits. Not a bad day, after all.

Makes 10 to 12 biscuits.

Ingredients

2 cups flour
2 teaspoons baking powder
1 teaspoon salt
3 tablespoons margarine,
   melted
1¼ cups milk

Materials

Large mixing bowl
Sifter
Tablespoon (for stirring),
   2 teaspoons
Cookie sheet

1 Sift together flour, baking powder, and salt in a large mixing bowl (see sifting tip on page 30).

2 Stir in melted margarine and milk until blended.

3 Using 2 teaspoons, carefully drop batter by spoonful onto a greased cookie sheet.

4 Bake at 450 degrees for 12 to 15 minutes, or until golden brown.

5 Serve piping hot from the oven, or split and toast them later. Yum!

Tip: You can melt the margarine in the microwave: put it into a microwave-safe cup, add 2 or 3 tablespoons of water, and microwave on high for half a minute. Check it and, if not melted completely, microwave for another half a minute. Let stand a few minutes, and be careful—it's HOT!

Terrific Toasted Cinnamon Rolls

Hunter Harris stops by on his bike, and he is so-o-o cute (and reckless—you saw him popping wheelies)! You chat a little, and then run out of things to say. Try, "Hungry? Let's make snacks!" Works every time.

Makes 8 rolls.

Ingredients

1 8-ounce can refrigerated
  crescent rolls
¼ cup brown sugar
2 tablespoons cinnamon
¼ cup raisins

Materials

Cookie sheet
Small bowl
Spoon (for mixing)

1 Unroll dough, separating into 8 triangles, and place on lightly greased cookie sheet (see greasing tip on page 17).

2 In a small bowl, mix together sugar and cinnamon and sprinkle on each dough shape.

3 Top with raisins, and roll up into loose crescents or round shapes. Pinch shut.

4 Bake at 375 degrees for 12 minutes, or until toasty brown.

Tip: Make sure that the dough is chilled: the warmer it is, the stickier it is.

Nutty Cheese Sticks

The best part of family reunions is the food. How about those nutty cheese sticks that your cousin Harriet brought all the way from Baltimore? They were so good, everyone asked her for the recipe.

Makes about 2 dozen sticks.

Ingredients

½ cup butter, softened
1 cup flour
½ teaspoon salt
2 cups Cheddar cheese, grated
1 cup pecans, chopped

Materials

Large mixing bowl
Waxed paper (optional)
Rolling pin
Knife
Cookie sheet

1 In a large bowl, mix together butter, flour, and salt; then add grated cheese (see grated cheese tip on page 15) and nuts.

2 On top of a clean and dry counter, or on a sheet of waxed paper, sprinkle a thin layer of flour (to prevent the dough from sticking).

3 Roll the dough onto the floured surface and shape into a ball. Using a rolling pin, roll out dough to about ½-inch thickness.

4 Cut into 2-inch strips and bake on greased cookie sheet (see greasing tip on page 17) at 350 degrees for about 10 minutes. Cool before serving.

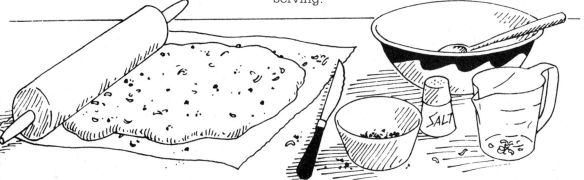

Tips: • Just as you can buy cheese already grated, you can also buy nuts already chopped.
• To soften butter, take it out of the refrigerator a few hours before you will need to use it and leave it on the counter (in the wrapper).
• If you don't have a rolling pin, you can use a long bottle or glass jar to roll the dough.

Give-Away Zucchini Bread

"Stop tapping your pencil!"
"Keep your hands to yourself!"
"Eyes on the board, and not on your neighbor!"
Wish your teacher would lighten up? A little bribery never hurt. That's why
Give-Away Zucchini Bread was invented!

Makes 2 loaves.

Ingredients

3 eggs
1 cup vegetable oil
2 cups sugar
2 cups zucchini, peeled
  and grated
1 teaspoon vanilla
3 cups flour
2 teaspoons cinnamon
1 teaspoon baking soda
1 teaspoon salt
¼ teaspoon baking powder
1 cup walnuts, chopped

Materials

Electric mixer
2 large mixing bowls
Grater (for the zucchini)
2 9-by-5-inch loaf pans
Toothpick (for testing
  doneness)

1 Using electric mixer, beat eggs in large mixing bowl until foamy.

2 Add oil, sugar, zucchini and vanilla.

3 In a separate bowl, mix together flour, cinnamon, baking soda, salt, and baking powder; then add to creamed mixture. Fold in chopped nuts.

4 Pour into 2 greased loaf pans (see greasing tip on page 17). Bake at 325 degrees for 1 hour, or until a toothpick inserted into the center of the loaf comes out clean (if the dough is not fully cooked, it will stick to the toothpick).

Tip: These make great holiday gifts for teachers and neighbors. Wrap in plastic wrap with a pretty ribbon. Don't give them all away, though. They're so good, you'll want to freeze some to eat later!

Sure-to-Please Banana Muffins

You saw the moving van unloading furniture across the street and noticed a girl's bike just like yours! Let's go meet the new neighbor—maybe she'd like a banana muffin break. And next time you'll invite her over to help you bake!

Makes 1 dozen muffins.

Ingredients

1¾ cups flour
2 teaspoons baking powder
½ teaspoon baking soda
¼ teaspoon salt
⅓ cup sugar
3 tablespoons butter, melted
1 egg, slightly beaten
1 cup ripe bananas, mashed

Materials

Large bowl
Medium bowl
Large spoon
Muffin tins

1 In a large bowl, sift together the first 5 ingredients (see sifting tip on page 30).

2 Combine the butter, egg, and bananas in a medium bowl and stir into the dry ingredients. Mix well.

3 Spoon batter into 12 greased muffin tins and bake at 400 degrees for 20 minutes.

Tip: You might want to line the muffin tins with paper muffin liners (you can buy them in any supermarket). That way you don't have to butter the tin cups and can just pop the baked muffin (in the liner) out of the tin cup—a ready-made holder.

Strawberry Surprise Snackin' Muffins

SHHHH!

The bake sale is tomorrow, and you really want to shine. So you pull out all the stops. Everyone will say, "Oh, tell us how you made these." But no-o-o, these jelly-filled treats are your specialty—and your secret. Let 'em eat their hearts out!

Makes 1 dozen muffins.

Ingredients

1 egg, slightly beaten with a fork
⅔ cup milk
¼ cup butter or margarine, melted (see melting tip on page 18)
1½ cups flour
½ cup sugar
1 cup fresh or frozen straw-berries, chopped
3 teaspoons baking powder
¼ teaspoon salt
¾ cup strawberry jam

Materials

2 large bowls
Sifter
Knife, large spoon, teaspoon
Muffin tins

1 In large bowl, combine egg, milk, and butter.

2 In a separate bowl, sift together flour, sugar, baking powder, and salt and add to egg mix-ture; then fold in chopped strawberries.

3 Spoon about 1 tablespoon batter into each of 12 greased muffin cups, and drop a teaspoon of strawberry jam into center of each.

4 Cover jam with remaining batter. Bake at 400 degrees for 15 to 20 minutes, or until golden brown.

Tip: Sifting (pouring the flour through a special container with very small holes) is done to distribute the baking powder well. Sifting also makes the flour fluffier, which will make the baked dough fluffier. But if you don't have a sifter, just be sure to mix the flour with the baking powder and the salt as thoroughly as possible before adding the wet stuff.

Rootin'-Tootin'-Cowboy Corn Muffins

You scraped your knee during a wild game of Cowboys and Indians. It really hurt, but you managed to keep a stiff upper lip. Your mom didn't even get mad at you for running in the house, and she let you help her make corn muffins—your favorite snack (when you're in need of some T.L.C.). Wow, those muffins really do make you feel better!

Makes 8 to 10 muffins.

Ingredients

1 cup milk
¼ cup vegetable oil
1 egg, slightly beaten with
   a fork
1 cup yellow corn meal
1 cup flour
4 teaspoons baking powder
2 tablespoons sugar
½ teaspoon salt

Materials

Large bowl
Medium bowl
Large spoon
Muffin tins

1 In a large bowl, beat together milk, oil, and egg with a fork.

2 Combine corn meal, flour, baking powder, sugar, and salt in a medium bowl; then fold into egg mixture.

3 Spoon batter into greased muffin tins or paper muffin cups (see greasing tip on page 17). Bake at 400 degrees for about 20 minutes, or until golden brown. Great when served hot with honey!

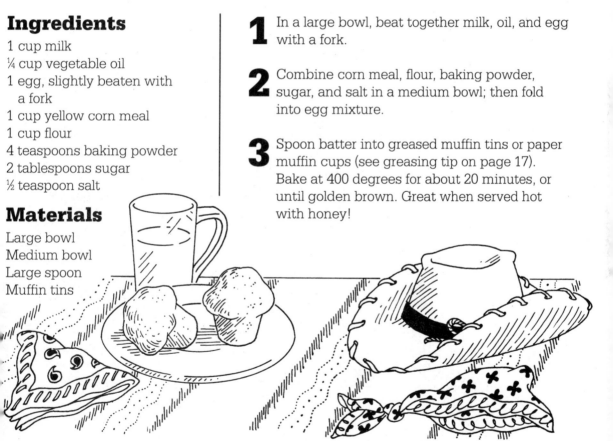

Tip: If you are using paper muffin cups, you should still put them into muffin tins— the paper cups are not very strong and will droop (and the muffins will look funny).

Happy-Face Raisin Bagels

Express yourself.
Explore your inner child.
Interpret your dreams.
Decorate a bagel.

Each bagel serves 1 person.

Ingredients

1 bagel, split and toasted
Cream cheese, softened
6 raisins
2 apple slices, cut into
  crescent shapes

Materials

Toaster (for bagels)
Butter knife (for cream
  cheese)
Knife (for slicing apple)
Plate

1 Put split bagel on a plate and spread each bagel half with cream cheese.

2 Press raisins and apple slices into the cream cheese to create a face (raisins for eyes and nose, and apple slice for the smile).

Tip: Be creative—you can also use chopped nuts to "draw" the smile, or use sliced maraschino cherries, mandarin oranges, and pineapple bits to create colorful designs.

SPECIAL
SNACKS

Peanut Buttery Granola Crunch

Your mom said that the last time she made granola, she was wearing tie-dye T-shirts and bell-bottoms. (You've seen the pictures—she did look pretty funny!) She says that not only do you dress better than she did, but that this granola is tastier because it's made with peanut butter—your favorite food!

Makes a large bowl—about 6 cups.

Ingredients

2 cups rolled oatmeal
½ cup wheat germ
½ cup coconut, grated
½ cup nuts, chopped
½ teaspoon salt
1 cup peanut butter
½ cup honey
2 tablespoons vegetable oil
1 cup raisins

Materials

Large bowl
Medium bowl
Cookie sheet or baking pan
Spoon (for mixing)

1 In a large bowl, combine first 4 ingredients.

2 In a medium bowl, mix together salt, peanut butter, honey, and oil; then fold gently into the oatmeal mixture.

3 Spread on a cookie sheet or in a baking pan. Bake at 300 degrees for 45 minutes, or until crisp and golden.

4 Let the granola cool a bit, and then stir to break up into munchable pieces. Mix in raisins.

Tip: If you are using salted nuts and peanut butter, you may want to leave out the salt, so your granola won't be too salty.

Explorer's Trail Mix

You're going on a very long hike and you'll need some nourishment. (Okay, okay, it's just to your special hideaway behind the garage. But you *will* need a snack.) How about whipping up some trail mix? Let the adventures begin....

Makes 8 cups.

Ingredients

4 cups cereal (wheat squares
    such as Wheat Chex® and
    round oats such as Cheerios®
    work well)
1 cup thin pretzel sticks
1 cup peanuts
2 tablespoons vegetable oil
1 tablespoon Worcestershire
    sauce
1 cup raisins
1 cup dried apples or apricots

Materials

Shallow baking pan
Small bowl
Large spoon (for stirring)

1 Spread cereal, pretzels, and peanuts in pan.

2 In a small bowl, mix together oil and Worcestershire sauce; then sprinkle the cereal mixture with the oil mix.

3 Bake at 350 degrees for about 10 minutes, or until toasted.

4 Cool; stir in raisins and dried fruit.

Tip: If you don't like peanuts, use other nuts—almonds, walnuts, or whatever your fancy.

Crisp-and-Chewy Cereal Squares

Legos.®
Slinkies.®
Hula Hoops.®
You're into the basics.
Even with your snack food.
Especially with your snack food.

Makes 2 dozen squares.

Ingredients

¼ cup margarine
1 10-ounce package regular
   marshmallows
6 cups crisp rice cereal
   (such as Rice Krispies® or
   similar generic brands)

Materials

Large saucepan
Large spoon (for stirring)
9-by-2-inch baking pan
Knife

1 In a large saucepan over low heat, melt margarine and stir in marshmallows until melted and blended.

2 Remove from heat and carefully fold in cereal, stirring until cereal is well coated.

3 Press into a greased pan (see greasing tip on page 17) and cool before cutting into 2-inch squares.

Tip: If you want, you can add 1 cup chocolate chips or peanut butter morsels during the second step.

No-Bake Oatmeal Drops

Waiting for the school bus. Christina says she has pudding in her lunch box. Jeffrey brought fruit. And you fixed your favorite oatmeal drops. Maybe you'll have just one little bite now?

Makes 2 to 3 dozen cookies.

Ingredients

2 cups sugar
3 tablespoons unsweetened
   cocoa powder
¼ teaspoon salt
1 stick butter or margarine
½ cup milk
3 cups quick-cooking oats

Materials

Large saucepan
Large spoon (for stirring)
Teaspoon
Waxed paper

1 In large saucepan over medium-to-high heat, combine sugar, cocoa, salt, butter, and milk; stir until mixture comes to a boil (see milk-boiling tip on page 2).

2 Remove from heat and stir in oatmeal.

3 Drop by teaspoonful onto waxed paper. Cookies will set as they cool.

Tip: Oatmeal is so-o-o good for you. It supplies fiber for smooth digestion.

Hoppin' Poppin' Caramel Corn

Watching the Super Bowl, and your pal Jerry won't stop talking. He tells jokes during the kick-off, chats over the instant replay, and even turns the channel in the middle of the cheerleader close-ups. Here, Jerry, this caramel corn should keep you quiet.

Makes a large bowl of popcorn.

Ingredients

1 bag microwave popcorn
½ cup butter
1 cup corn syrup

Materials

Microwave
Large bowl
Medium saucepan
Large spoon (for stirring)

1 Pop popcorn according to package instructions and pour into a large bowl.

2 In a saucepan, over low heat, heat together butter and corn syrup until melted.

3 Pour over popped popcorn and stir.

Tip: For variety, add ½ cup peanuts or chocolate chips in Step 3.

Raisin Ants on Celery Logs

Ahh…the joys of a picnic in the park. You pack a basket full of goodies and a cozy blanket to sit on. You can even bring along your own ants! (Raisin ants, that is!)

Serves 2 to 3 people.

Ingredients

2 celery stalks
½ cup peanut butter
Raisins

Materials

Knife

1 Cut each celery stalk into halves or thirds and fill insides with peanut butter.

2 Sprinkle raisins on top, for the "ants."

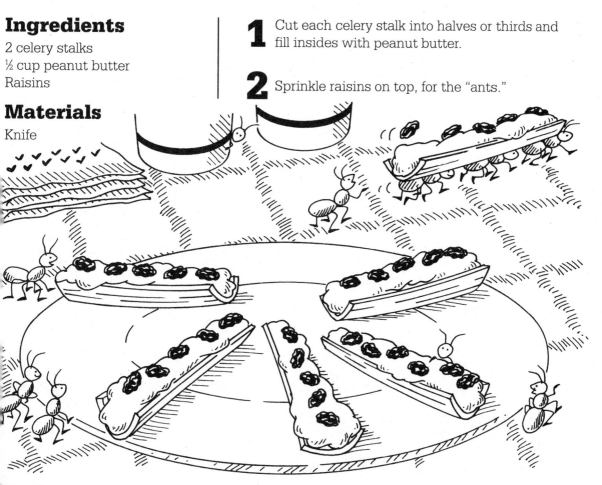

Tip: You may want to try cream cheese topped with pineapple bits or olive slices as another yummy filling.

Carrot Sticks with Confetti Dip

Good-bye, tofu. Hello, veggies! Snacks don't have to taste like cardboard in order to be healthy. Try this cool and colorful snack, and see if you don't agree!

Makes about 2 cups of dip.

Ingredients

½ cup sour cream
½ cup mayonnaise
¼ cup grated Parmesan
  cheese
¼ cup red bell pepper,
  chopped
¼ cup cucumber, chopped
Sprinkle of garlic salt
Carrot sticks, washed,
  peeled, and sliced

Materials

Knife (for chopping)
Cutting board
Large bowl
Large spoon (for mixing)

1 In a large bowl, mix together everything except carrots.

2 Serve chilled with carrot sticks.

Tip: In a hurry? Try dipping carrot and celery sticks in peanut butter. You'll love it!

Wiggly-Squiggly Gelatin Shapes

It's a snack!
It's a toy!
You can pick it up, play with it, then eat it!
What more could you ask for?

Serves 12 people.

Ingredients

1 ounce (4 envelopes)
   unflavored gelatin
4 cups fruit juice

Materials

Large mixing bowl
Large spoon (for stirring)
Medium saucepan
9-by-13-inch pan
Cookie cutters or knife

1 In a large mixing bowl, stir together gelatin with 1 cup juice until well mixed.

2 In a saucapan, heat remaining 3 cups of fruit juice and add the hot juice to the gelatin mixture; mix until completely dissolved.

3 Pour into pan and refrigerate until firm.

4 Use cookie cutters to make wiggly shapes, or use a knife to cut into squares for serving.

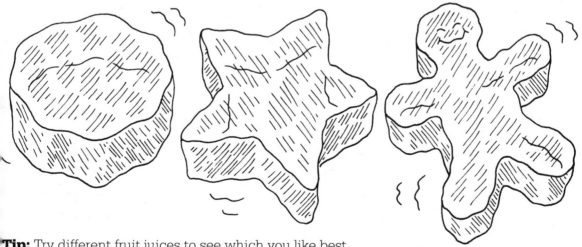

Tip: Try different fruit juices to see which you like best.

Famous Frozen Banana Pops

The best things at the zoo were the monkeys (they were so funny) and the frozen banana treats (they were yummy). Try whipping them up at home with your friends, and you'll have more fun than a barrel of monkeys!

Makes 4 snacks.

Ingredients

2 large bananas
1 cup chocolate chips
2 tablespoons water

Material

Knife
4 wooden skewers
Small saucepan (or
 microwave-safe dish and
 microwave)
Large spoon (for stirring)
Waxed paper
Aluminum foil

1 Peel bananas and cut each in half to get 4 short, stocky banana halves. Insert skewers through cut bottoms of bananas.

2 In a small saucepan over low heat on stovetop (or in a microwave-safe dish in the microwave), melt chocolate chips with water. (If you are melting the chips in the microwave, heat for 1 minute, and stir. Repeat as many times as you need until the chips are melted.)

3 Dip bananas in chocolate and cool on waxed paper until set.

4 Once the chocolate cover is firm, wrap the dipped bananas in aluminum foil and freeze until serving.

Tip: You can also roll the dipped bananas in chopped nuts or coconut before freezing. Yum!

Frozen Fruit-'N'-Juicy Bars

A game of hide-and-seek on a summer night. You're working very hard to stay hidden, and it's not easy to sit still with mosquitoes biting at your ankles. Where is everyone? You tiptoe up to the kitchen window, and there they are, grabbing fruit pops from the freezer while you're still out in the dark! Better hurry in before the snacks are all gone!

Makes about 6 pops.

Ingredients

2 cups orange juice
1 tablespoon lemon juice
1 8-ounce can crushed
    pineapple with juice
1 banana, chopped into small
    bits
1 2-ounce jar maraschino
    cherries, drained

Materials

Large bowl
Knife
6 small waxed paper cups
6 wooden popsicle sticks

1 Mix juices and fruit together in a large bowl.

2 Pour into waxed paper cups and place in freezer.

3 When the popsicles are partially frozen, place a popsicle stick in center of each cup.

4 Continue freezing until firm. Peel off cups to serve.

Tip: For a faster treat, use your favorite prepared drink mix and freeze in plastic ice-cube trays.

Deliciously Devilish Hard-Cooked Eggs

Which came first, the chicken or the egg? (Munch while you contemplate.)

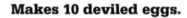

Makes 10 deviled eggs.

Ingredients

5 eggs
¼ cup mayonnaise
1 teaspoon mustard
Salt and pepper, to taste
Paprika

Materials

Medium saucepan with lid
Knife, fork, spoon
Small bowl

1 Place eggs in saucepan full of water and bring to boil.

2 Cover the saucepan with the lid and reduce heat to simmer, cooking for another 15 to 20 minutes. Pour off the water and rinse the eggs; then cool.

3 Peel eggs and cut in half lengthwise. Carefully remove yolks and place in small bowl. Mash with fork and add mayonnaise, mustard, salt, and pepper; then spoon into egg-white halves.

4 Sprinkle tops with paprika; chill.

Tip: If you rinse the eggs with cold water in Step 2, the shell should come off easier.

Cheesy Salsa and Nifty Nachos

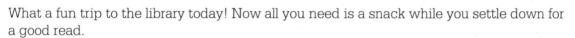

A Wrinkle in Time.
The Wind in the Willows.
Charlotte's Web.
The Lion, the Witch, and the Wardrobe.

What a fun trip to the library today! Now all you need is a snack while you settle down for a good read.

Makes a bunch of snacks.

Ingredients

1-pound package processed
   American cheese
1 8-ounce jar salsa
Tortilla chips
½ to 1 cup tomatoes, chopped
½ cup olives, chopped

Materials

Knife
Cutting board
Large microwave-safe bowl
Microwave

1 On a cutting board, chop cheese into small cubes and place in large microwave-safe bowl.

2 Add salsa and heat in microwave for 2 to 3 minutes, or until melted.

3 Put the tortilla chips on a large plate and pour the cheese-salsa mixture over tortilla chips.

4 Top with tomatoes and olives (you can use more or less chopped tomatoes and olives, depending on what you like).

Tips: You can also try piling chips on a plate, sprinkling them with cheese cubes, salsa, chopped tomatoes, and chopped olives, and then microwaving the whole thing—this way everything melts on top of the cheese and the flavors combine really well. Try both ways to see which one you like best. And have plenty of napkins ready—or just lick your fingers!

A Bunch of Lunch

Kid-Sized Pizza Rounds

Slam-dunk.
Home run.
A+.
She likes you.
Ever had one of those days where everything goes right? Oh, go ahead, admit it. You were brilliant today! Treat yourself. You deserve it!

Allow 2 muffin halves per serving.

Ingredients

English muffins, split into
   halves
1 jar pizza or spaghetti sauce
Mozzarella cheese, grated
Pepperoni slices
Green peppers, chopped
Mushrooms, sliced

Materials

Cookie sheet or baking dish
Knife (for chopping)
Cutting board

1 Place split muffins on a cookie sheet, top muffin halves with pizza sauce, and cover with cheese.

2 Layer additional ingredients on top of cheese. Bake at 375 degrees for about 10 minutes.

Tip: The amounts of the toppings depend on how many servings you are making and on what you like best. After all, this is your treat, so pile on your favorites! Be adventurous and think up some other delicious toppings!

Pick-'Em-Up Pigs in the Blanket

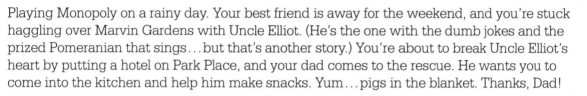

Playing Monopoly on a rainy day. Your best friend is away for the weekend, and you're stuck haggling over Marvin Gardens with Uncle Elliot. (He's the one with the dumb jokes and the prized Pomeranian that sings...but that's another story.) You're about to break Uncle Elliot's heart by putting a hotel on Park Place, and your dad comes to the rescue. He wants you to come into the kitchen and help him make snacks. Yum...pigs in the blanket. Thanks, Dad!

Makes 10 pigs in the blanket.

Ingredients

1 tube of 10 ready-to-bake
    biscuits
5 frankfurters
Mustard
Ketchup

Materials

Knife
Cookie sheet or shallow
    baking pan

1 Cut frankfurters in half cross-wise.

2 Wrap a biscuit around each half and place on ungreased baking sheet. Bake at 400 degrees for about 10 minutes, or until crusts are golden brown.

3 Serve warm and dip in mustard or ketchup.

Tip: If the "blankets" don't want to stay together, use toothpicks to keep them in place.

Tasty Tuna-and-Cheese Boats

Your art teacher says you've got a good eye.
And your girlfriend says you've got good taste.
Let's see what you can do with this good-looking, tasty version of a tuna sandwich!

Makes 4 tuna boats.

Ingredients

1 6-ounce can tuna, drained
2 tablespoons sweet pickle
   relish
2 tablespoons mayonnaise
2 hot dog buns, split
2 slices American cheese

Materials

Medium mixing bowl
Large spoon (for mixing)
Knife (for spreading and
   slicing)
4 toothpicks

1 In a mixing bowl, stir together tuna, pickle relish, and mayonnaise. Spread on top of the 4 open-faced bun halves.

2 Slice each cheese square diagonally to form 2 triangles out of each slice (4 triangles in total). Insert toothpick into shortest side of triangle and stick into tuna boat to form sail.

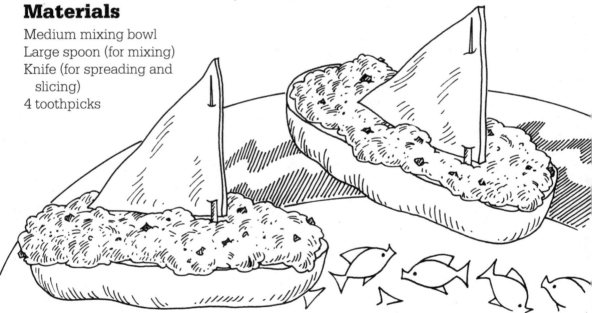

Tip: Always choose water-packed tuna instead of oil-packed. It's so much healthier for you—and tastes better, too.

Super-Duper Sloppy Joes

I like coffee,
I like tea.
I'd like Susannah,
To jump rope with me.

A new friend. You invite her to lunch, and make your very favorite, very special Sloppy Joes.

Makes 8 Sloppy Joes.

Ingredients

1½ pounds lean ground beef
½ cup onion, minced
½ cup green pepper, chopped
Salt and pepper, to taste
¾ cup tomato sauce
8 sandwich buns, toasted

Materials

Large skillet
Wooden spoon (for stirring)
Large spoon
Toaster
Knife (for chopping)
Cutting board

1 In a large skillet over medium heat, brown ground beef with onion and green pepper, stirring until the beef is cooked (it should not be pink at all).

2 Drain grease; sprinkle with salt and pepper; and stir in tomato sauce, simmering until heated throughout.

3 Spoon beef mixture into toasted sandwich buns.

Tip: You can use ground turkey instead of ground beef—the taste is the same, and the Sloppy Joes will be healthier and lower in fat.

Really Good Grilled Cheese Sandwich

Saturday is allowance day, but chores have to be done before you collect.

1. Clean your room.
2. Take out the garbage.
3. Sweep the garage.
4. Rake the leaves (and it's the middle of October).

Finally, you get your pay-off. Even though your cousin Herbert (who is the same age) gets twice as much, you're too tired to bring it up...and too hungry!

Makes 1 sandwich.

Ingredients

2 slices bread
2 slices American cheese
1 tablespoon margarine,
  softened (see softening tip
  on page 31)

Materials

Butter knife (for spreading)
Skillet
Spatula

1 Place cheese between 2 slices of bread and spread outside surfaces of bread with the margarine.

2 In preheated skillet, cook sandwich on medium to low heat. Turn frequently with spatula for 5 to 10 minutes, or until bread is golden and cheese is melted.

Tip: You can add ham, turkey, or cooked bacon slices to your sandwich together with the cheese...so good!

Simply Scrumptious Sandwich Shapes

Invite your friends for lunch.
Cute table linens.
Cute outfit.
And of course, something cute to eat.

Makes however much you want.

1 Use cookie cutters to cut sandwich bread into your favorite shapes, or try other breads:

    bagels
    raisin bread
    rice cakes
    pita pockets
    English muffins

2 For fillings, let your imagination go wild:

    peanut butter and honey
    apple butter and marshmallow creme
    cream cheese and apple slices
    pimiento cheese and bacon
    chopped egg and celery with mayonnaise

3 Top with sprinkles of colorful garnishes:

    raisins and coconut
    pickles and olives
    bean sprouts and avocado
    cherry tomatoes and lettuce leaves
    green pepper and carrot slices

Tip: No combination is too strange, as long as you like it!

Foot-Long Submarine Sandwich

Your next-door neighbor, Guthrie, is a very big guy. He's the running back for the football team, and is 8 feet tall (give or take a few inches). They say he drinks 2 gallons of milk and eats 3 sandwiches every day at the school cafeteria. You've got to see it to believe it, and invite him over for lunch. What should you serve? Oh, Guthrie, do you like submarine sandwiches?

Makes 6 to 8 sandwiches.

Ingredients

1 loaf French bread, sliced
½ cup mayonnaise
2 teaspoons mustard
1 2-ounce jar chopped
   pimientos
6 to 8 slices cooked ham
6 to 8 slices Swiss cheese
Lettuce, pickles, and chips
   for garnish

Materials

Aluminum foil
Medium bowl
Knife (for spreading)
Serving plate

1 Place sliced bread loaf on large piece of aluminum foil.

2 Combine mayonnaise, mustard, and pimientos in a bowl; spread mixture between every other slice of bread.

3 Fold ham and cheese slices in half diagonally, and insert into openings that were spread with mayonnaise mixture.

4 Wrap loaf in foil, and bake at 350 degrees for 30 minutes, or until heated throughout.

5 Place on a plate on a bed of lettuce and surround with pickles and chips.

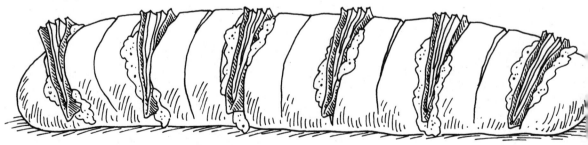

Tip: Experiment with cheeses and lunch meats until you find your favorite combination.

Roll-'Em-Up Ham and Cheese Bites

"Knock, knock."
"Who's there?"
"Orange."
"Orange who?"
"Orange you glad your mom packed your favorite ham roll-ups in your lunch box today?"

Serves 6 (2 roll-ups per serving).

Ingredients

2 tablespoons mustard
2 tablespoons mayonnaise
12 slices packaged ham
12 slices Swiss or American
    cheese
12 sticks celery, cut into
    same length as ham slices

Materials

1 small bowl
Large spoon (for mixing)
Knife (for spreading)
Toothpicks
Plate

1 In a small bowl, mix together mustard and mayonnaise; spread on ham slices.

2 Top each ham slice with a cheese slice and roll around celery; secure each roll with a toothpick.

3 Arrange on a plate and munch!

Tip: And the roll-up tastes not half-bad with an asparagus spear in the middle, instead of celery.

Mexican Jumping Bean and Cheese Quesadillas

You're adventurous.
You're sophisticated.
And you're hungry.
So this south-of-the-border version of a grilled cheese sandwich is the perfect snack for you.
Olé!

Allow 1 quesadilla per serving.

Ingredients

Flour tortillas, 2 per person
1 can refried beans
Cheddar or Monterey Jack
   cheese, grated
1 jar salsa

Materials

Knife or spoon (for spreading)
Skillet
Spatula
Plate

1 For each quesadilla, spread about 2 tablespoons refried beans on a tortilla and place face up in preheated greased skillet.

2 Sprinkle about ¼ cup cheese on beans, and place another tortilla on top. Press down with spatula.

3 Cook on medium heat, turning carefully to brown both sides until filling is hot and cheese is melted.

4 Transfer to a plate and cut into fourths. Dip in salsa for a south-of-the-border taste.

Tip: Optional items to add to filling are chopped tomatoes, black olives, and sour cream.

Soups, Salads, and Stuff

Comforting Creamy Potato Soup

You're home with the sniffles, and you don't even feel like watching your favorite episode of *I Love Lucy!* But Aunt Rhoda comes bustling over with her famous potato soup, which she says is a cure for colds, the flu, or just the plain old blahs. It tastes so good, you ask for more. Then you reach for the remote control to see what Lucy and Ricky are up to.

Makes 4 servings.

Ingredients

2 cups canned chicken broth
3 potatoes, peeled and
    chopped into small pieces
4 green onions, chopped
½ cup celery, chopped
1 teaspoon salt
2 cups milk

Materials

Large saucepan
Knife (for chopping)
Masher or fork
Large spoon (for stirring)
Ladle
4 bowls
4 soup spoons

1 Pour chicken broth into large saucepan, and add potatoes, onions, celery, and salt.

2 Bring to a boil; then lower heat and simmer for 30 to 45 minutes, or until potatoes are soft.

3 With a masher or a fork, mash potatoes in the soup and add milk. Stir over low heat, just until milk is warm.

4 Ladle into bowls and eat.

Tip: This soup is great with a sprinkle of grated cheese or bacon bits on top!

Go-Fishing Tomato Soup

Learning all about dinosaurs in school.
The ones who are plant-eaters. (They're dumb.)
The ones who are meat-eaters. (They're scary.)
The ones who are soup-eaters. (Just kidding!)
If I were a dinosaur, I would be Tomato-soup-o-saurus.
I like it any time, any place, any which way.

Makes 4 servings.

Ingredients

3 cups tomato juice
4 tablespoons onions, minced
2 tablespoons parsley
½ teaspoon basil
½ teaspoon salt
1 cup milk
Goldfish cheese crackers

Materials

Mincer (for the onions)
Large saucepan
Large spoon (for stirring)
Ladle
4 bowls
4 soup spoons

1 Combine tomato juice with onions and spices in a saucepan over medium high heat. Bring to a boil, stirring occasionally.

2 Lower heat; add milk and stir until creamy and warm. (Don't let the milk boil, or it will form a skin on the top.)

3 Ladle into bowls and sprinkle goldfish crackers into soup. Use your spoon to go fishing for the crackers! It's okay to swallow these goldfish!

Tip: If you don't have a mincer, chop the onions very small and then squish them with a fork.

Hearty and Healthy Veggie Soup

So you lost a tooth last night, and the Tooth Fairy put a parking token under your pillow, instead of a silver dollar. Your mom assures you that it was probably an accident; that the Tooth Fairy can't see very well in the dark, and that she's sure the situation will be corrected immediately! In the meantime, your mouth is sore, so you need to eat something mushy, like soup. Maybe you can help chop the carrots.

Makes 4 bowls of soup.

Ingredients

1 10-ounce can beef broth
2 cups water
1 cup corn kernels, canned or
    frozen
1 cup carrots, chopped
1 cup potatoes, chopped
1 cup tomatoes, chopped
1 teaspoon thyme
2 teaspoons salt
1 teaspoon pepper

Materials

Knife and cutting board (for
    chopping)
Large saucepan
Large spoon (for stirring)
Ladle
4 bowls
4 soup spoons

1 Combine all ingredients together in a large saucepan over medium high heat, and bring to a boil.

2 Reduce heat and simmer, stirring occasionally, for about an hour, or until vegetables are tender.

3 Ladle into soup bowls.

Tip: Just about any vegetable works well in this soup. You can also try chopped cabbage, canned beans, celery chunks, or onions.

Ask-for-More Carrot and Raisin Salad

Summer vacation at the beach. Morning walks to find seashells, afternoons building sand castles, and leisurely evenings with cool salad suppers. Can we make carrot-and-raisin salad tonight?

Makes 2 servings.

Ingredients

2 carrots
1 teaspoon lemon juice
¼ teaspoon salt
¾ cup raisins
⅓ cup mayonnaise

Materials

Vegetable peeler
Large serving bowl
Grater
Large spoon (for stirring)

1 Wash carrots and scrape with vegetable peeler.

2 In large serving bowl, grate the carrots into large slivers: then sprinkle with lemon juice and salt.

3 Stir raisins and mayonnaise into the carrots. Serve.

Tips: It's fun to learn new kitchen skills. For shredding and grating vegetables, you can use a grater...but be careful not to nick your fingers!

Especially Festive Melon Boats

Picking berries with your grandfather. He apologizes for being so slow. He says it's getting harder and harder to bend over lately, but you can take over now, because he's taught you all his tricks—like how to spot the best berries, and how to avoid the prickly parts. You're such a pro that your bucket fills up really fast. You can't wait to get back and show Grandma.

Each melon half serves one person.

Ingredients

1 cantaloupe melon
1 cup blueberries
1 cup strawberries
1 cup pineapple chunks
1 cup sliced peaches
1 cup green or red seedless
   grapes

Materials

Knife, spoon
Medium bowl

1 Cut cantaloupe in half and scoop out seeds. Then scoop out cantaloupe into a bowl and cut into bite-sized pieces.

2 Add remaining fruit to cantaloupe chunks, and place all the fruit into the melon shells.

Tip: If you have any fruit left over, make more boats or eat later as a fruit salad. This fruit salad also looks pretty when served in a scooped-out pineapple shell or on a bed of lettuce.

Very-Cherry Gelatin Cups

Did you know that when George Washington chopped down the cherry tree, he wasn't sent to bed without his supper—because he told the truth! And because he created a wiggly cherry dish for his dad (or so they say).

Makes 6 servings.

Ingredients

1 6-ounce package instant
  cherry gelatin
2 cups boiling water
2 cups cold water
1 16-ounce can tart pitted
  cherries, drained
1 cup miniature marshmallows

Materials

Large bowl
Large spoon (for stiring)
6 glass dishes

1 Combine gelatin and boiling water in a large bowl; stir until well mixed.

2 Add cold water. Pour the gelatin into individual glass dishes and place in refrigerator until lightly set—about 1 hour.

3 Fold cherries and marshmallows into the cooled gelatin and continue chilling until firm—about 3 hours.

Tip: If you like nuts, you can also add ½ cup of chopped pecans or walnuts together with the cherries and marshmallows in Step 3.

Garden-Fresh Tossed Green Salad

After a weekend at your aunt's house in the country, she loaded you with fresh vegetables from her garden. (She's famous for growing the best cucumbers in the county. You wish you had a relative famous for something more exciting than that.) If your auntie had been a millionaire instead of a gardener, she would have loaded you up with money. Anyway, it's your turn to make salad tonight. And you have to admit, the cucumbers are pretty good looking.

Makes as much as you like!

Ingredients

Lettuce, torn into bite-sized
    pieces
Tomatoes, chopped
Cucumbers, sliced
Celery, sliced
Any of your other favorite
    vegetables

Materials

Knife (for chopping and
    slicing)
Cutting board
Large salad bowl

1 Mix chilled, cut-up vegetables together in the salad bowl.

2 Top with your favorite salad dressing.

Tip: Use as much of each vegetable as you like for your own personal combination. Also, why not be a gourmet, and try different types of salad leaves, such as spinach, romaine, arugula, or curly endive, in your tossed salad?!

Tasty Tex-Mex Taco Salad

For tomorrow's covered dish lunch at school, you'll want to bring something that's light and tasty (and okay—it's Bryan Bagwell's favorite).
Buenos dias, Bryan!

Makes 4 servings.

Ingredients

½ pound lean ground beef
1 teaspoon chili powder
1 teaspoon salt
1 head of lettuce, shredded
2 tomatoes, chopped
1 cup cheese, grated
1 10-ounce package tortilla
   chips
1 15-ounce can kidney beans,
   drained
French salad dressing

Materials

Large skillet
Wooden spoon (for stirring)
Large salad bowl

1 In large skillet, cook ground beef with chili powder, stirring until browned. Drain grease, and sprinkle the beef with salt. Cool.

2 In salad bowl, combine lettuce, tomato, cheese, and chips, then toss in beef and beans.

3 Sprinkle with salad dressing.

Tip: If the ground beef is still hot when you add it to the rest of the ingredients, the lettuce will wilt.

Good-for-You Tuna-Stuffed Tomatoes

Field trip to the symphony. On the bus you sit next to Wanda Sue, who chatters nonstop about her allergies. Lunch afterward in the gallery buffet. You choose the stuffed tomato because it looks pretty. (And because you saw Marie-Helene—who is so-o sophisticated—put one on her plate.) Hmmm…It tastes pretty good. Maybe you'll grab the seat next to Marie-Helene on the way back.

Makes 2 stuffed tomatoes.

Ingredients

2 ripe tomatoes
1 7-ounce can chunk tuna in
  spring water, drained
¼ cup sweet pickle relish
¼ cup mayonnaise
Lettuce leaves

Materials

Knife, spoon
2 small bowls
2 plates

1 Wash the tomatoes; cut off the tops and scoop out seeds and pulp into a bowl (you can use the pulp for something else later).

2 In another bowl, mix together tuna, pickle relish, and mayonnaise.

3 Spoon tuna mixture into tomato shells, and place on plates covered with lettuce leaves.

Tip: If your tomatoes aren't quite ripe enough, you can put them in a brown paper bag in a dark place overnight, and the next day they'll be just right!

Dig In for Dinner

Catch-of-the-Day Fish Bake

"Row, Row, Row Your Boat."
"Popeye the Sailor Man."
The Old Man and the Sea.
Impress your family with your catch-of-the-day fish dish. It's guaranteed to make a splash!

Makes 4 servings.

Ingredients

4 fish fillets (sole, snapper, or orange roughy are good choices)
¼ cup butter, melted
4 teaspoons lemon juice
½ cup seasoned bread crumbs
¼ cup grated Parmesan cheese

Materials

Baking dish
Aluminum foil
Fork
4 plates

1 Place fish fillets in greased baking dish. Drizzle butter and lemon juice on top.

2 Sprinkle bread crumbs and cheese over fish.

3 Cover with foil and bake at 350 degrees for 45 minutes, or until fish is well-done and flakes with a fork.

4 Serve on plates with your favorite side dishes.

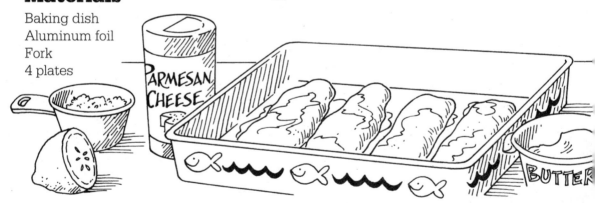

Tip: Be extra careful to make sure the fish is cooked completely. Cooked fish will be white and flaky and will not have the grayish-white color of raw fish. Uncooked fish can make you sick.

Ready-to-Dip Chicken Strips

Q. Why did the chicken cross the road?
A. To take a dip in the marmalade sauce!

Makes 4 servings.

Ingredients

4 boneless, skinless chicken
    breasts
1 cup flour
2 teaspoons salt
1 teaspoon pepper
½ cup vegetable oil
1 cup orange marmalade
2 teaspoons mustard

Materials

Cutting board
Knife
Plastic bag
Baking dish
Aluminum foil
Spatula
Microwave-safe dish
Microwave

1 On the cutting board, slice chicken breasts into narrow strips.

2 Mix together flour, salt, and pepper in a plastic bag. Add chicken and shake until coated with the flour mixture.

3 Pour oil into baking dish and place coated chicken in dish. Cover with foil and bake at 400 degrees for 40 minutes. Then turn the chicken with a spatula and bake uncovered for another 20 minutes, or until golden and crisp.

4 In a microwave-safe dish, combine marmalade and mustard. Heat in microwave for 1 minute and serve with chicken for dipping.

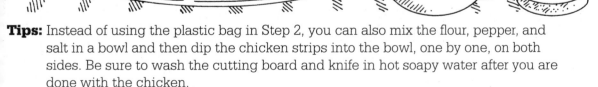

Tips: Instead of using the plastic bag in Step 2, you can also mix the flour, pepper, and salt in a bowl and then dip the chicken strips into the bowl, one by one, on both sides. Be sure to wash the cutting board and knife in hot soapy water after you are done with the chicken.

Chinese Chicken Stir-Fry

Did you ever notice that Opie's problems were always solved in 30 minutes? (They weren't that big, anyway…hitting a baseball into Aunt Bea's pie, or losing his pet cricket in Barney Fife's patrol car.) That was then. This is now. You flunked your math test today, and your parents won't be happy. Why don't you have dinner ready when they get home, so some of their surprises will be good ones?

Makes 4 to 6 servings.

Ingredients

1 pound boneless, skinless
   chicken breasts
3 tablespoons vegetable oil
1 cup broccoli, chopped
1 cup carrots, chopped
1 cup celery, chopped
1 5-ounce can sliced water
   chestnuts, drained
½ cup chicken broth
2 tablespoons corn starch
¼ cup soy sauce
1 tablespoon sugar
Rice, cooked

Materials

Cutting board
Knife
Large skillet or wok
Wooden spoon (for stirring)

1 On the cutting board, slice chicken into long thin strips.

2 Place oil in large skillet or wok over medium heat and cook chicken, stirring until it turns white.

3 Stir in vegetables and cook for a few minutes.

4 In small bowl, stir together corn starch and broth, then add soy sauce and sugar. Pour into skillet, stirring until sauce is thickened and vegetables are done (they should be a little soft, but still crunchy and not limp—taste them to be sure).

5 Serve mixture over cooked rice.

Tip: To cook rice, follow the instructions on the package. The general rule is 1 cup of white rice to 2 cups of water. Bring to a boil, then lower the heat, cover and cook until all water evaporates—about 20 minutes. Use a medium-to-large pot because 1 cup of raw rice will turn into 3 cups of cooked rice.

Smells-So-Good Mini Meat Loaves

"I know you are, but what am I?"
"Act your age, not your shoe size."
"Look at my thumb. Gee, you're dumb!"
Okay, so your family's not the Brady Bunch. Sometimes it's tough being the little brother. Help your mom make meat loaves for dinner tonight. They're so good that everyone will be impressed. That'll show 'em!

Makes 4 servings.

Ingredients

1 pound lean ground beef
1 egg, beaten
1 cup spaghetti sauce
½ cup bread crumbs
Salt and pepper, to taste

Materials

Large bowl
Muffin tins
Whisk or fork (to beat egg)
Large spoon (for mixing)

1 Preheat oven to 350 degrees.

2 Combine all ingredients in a large bowl and shape into 3-inch balls.

3 Place 1 ball into each greased muffin cup (see greasing tip on page 17) and bake at 350 degrees for 30 to 45 minutes, or until the meat is browned on the outside and no longer pink inside.

Tip: You can test doneness by sticking a fork into 1 of the loaves, after you take it out of the oven. If one of them is done, the rest should be done also.

Munchy-Crunchy Frito Pie

You had this Frito pie at the school cafeteria, and decided to try it at home. Your big brother, who's a vegetarian this week (last week he was on a French-fry diet) turns up his nose. After everyone has scraped their bowls clean, though, you see him in the kitchen helping himself to the leftovers. Humph! That didn't last long!

Makes 4 to 6 servings.

Ingredients

1 16-ounce can chili con carne
1 16-ounce can red kidney beans, drained
Corn chips (Frito or any other corn chips)
Cheddar cheese, grated

Materials

Large saucepan
Wooden spoon (for stirring)
4 or 6 serving bowls
Large spoon

1 Combine chili and beans in saucepan over medium heat, stirring until completely heated.

2 Layer corn chips in bottoms of serving bowls and spoon warm chili on top; then sprinkle with grated cheese.

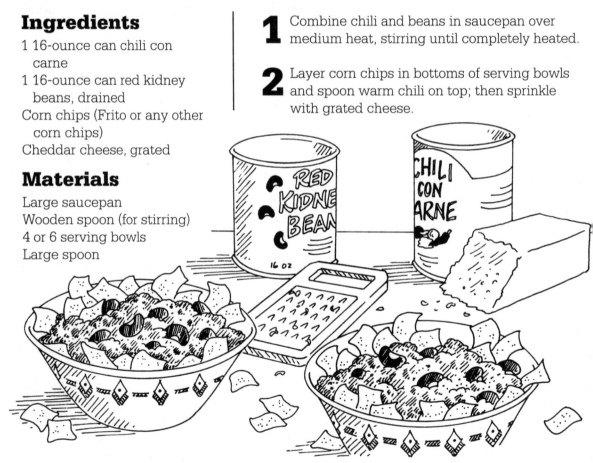

Tip: Turn this dish into a salad by adding chopped lettuce and tomato on top.

Mama Mia's Spaghetti with Meat Sauce

"On top of spaghetti, all covered with cheese,
I lost my poor meatball, when somebody sneezed.
It rolled off the table, and onto the floor.
It rolled through the kitchen, and out of the..."
You know the rest.

Makes 6 servings.

Ingredients

1 pound lean ground beef
2 15-ounce cans tomato
   sauce
1 cup water
2 tablespoons onion flakes
1 tablespoon brown sugar
1 teaspoon oregano
1 teaspoon salt
1 teaspoon basil
½ teaspoon garlic powder
1 12-ounce package of
  .spaghetti, cooked
Grated Parmesan cheese

Materials

Large saucepan
Wooden spoon (for stirring)
6 plates

1 Cook ground beef in large saucepan over medium heat, stirring until meat is brown and well-done.

2 Drain off grease and add sauce, water, and spices to the meat in the saucepan. Heat to boiling and simmer for a few minutes.

3 Divide cooked spaghetti among the plates and spoon sauce over spaghetti. Sprinkle Parmesan cheese on top.

Tip: Make the spaghetti according to package instructions. You might want to start the spaghetti right before you begin cooking the meat. If the spaghetti is ready before the sauce, drain off the water and cover the pot, to keep the spaghetti warm until the rest of the meal is ready.

Not-Just-for-Campout Beanie-Weenies

Legend has it that Tonto didn't like beans and franks—until he tasted the Lone Ranger's version. Try some, and see what you think!

Makes 6 servings.

Ingredients

2 21-ounce cans pork and
  beans
¾ cup ketchup
1 tablespoon mustard
2 tablespoons brown sugar
2 tablespoons onions, minced
6 to 8 frankfurters

Materials

Large bowl
Baking dish with cover
Knife

1 Preheat oven to 350 degrees.

2 Mix together first 5 ingredients in a bowl and pour into greased baking dish (see greasing tip on page 17).

3 Slice frankfurters into chunks and place on top of bean mixture.

4 Cover and bake at 350 degrees for 45 minutes. Remove cover for last 15 minutes to brown the franks.

Tip: Or serve your beanie-weenies on a bun. Place whole frankfurters into toasted hot dog buns and pour heated bean mixture over franks. Top with grated cheese. (It's super!)

Top-Your-Own Burgers

Sunday night is burger night. You always have burgers on Sunday nights. You get to help shape the patties, and when they're done, you get to choose your own toppings. It's your favorite meal of the week. Life is good!

Allow 1 burger per person.

Ingredients

1 pound lean ground beef
½ teaspoon salt
1 tablespoon Worcestershire sauce
1 tablespoon butter
4 hamburger buns, toasted or heated

Materials

Large bowl
Large skillet
Spatula

1 Mix meat with salt and Worcestershire sauce in a large bowl, and shape into 4 round patties.

2 Melt butter in a large skillet. Add patties, flipping with a spatula and cooking until meat is done, about 3 to 4 minutes on each side.

3 Serve in burger buns with your choice of toppings:

mayonnaise and mustard
ketchup
cheese slices
lettuce and tomato
pickles
sliced onion
cooked bacon

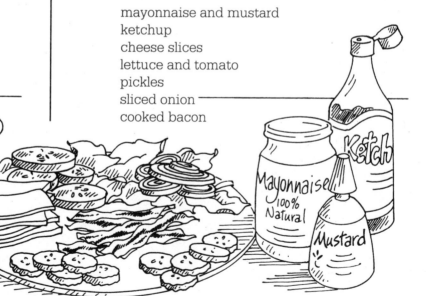

Tip (sort of): Did you know that the hamburger was named for the place where it was invented—Hamburg, Germany—and was brought to America by immigrants around 1850?

Veggies and Grains

Dippity-Do-Dah Broccoli Bites

You fed your breakfast to the dog. You crossed your eyes and held them there for thirty seconds. You drank out of the milk carton when no one was looking. And you didn't get caught! Now you owe it to your mom to eat some green vegetables tonight. Maybe some broccoli?

Makes 4 servings.

Ingredients

2 pounds broccoli
1 cup American cheese, grated
2 tablespoons butter or margarine
½ cup milk

Materials

Knife
Large pot
Medium saucepan
Medium bowl

1 Cut the stems off the broccoli and slice into small "flowerets." Place into a pot and cook uncovered, stem-side down, in boiling water for about 5 minutes.

2 In a separate saucepan over low heat (or in a microwave-safe dish in the microwave), melt cheese and butter in milk. Pour in bowl and serve as a dip or sauce with the cooked broccoli.

Tip: For a really creamy sauce, use processed cheeses—they melt really well.

Zippy Zucchini Sticks

Your soccer game didn't go so well. All right, admit it . . . it was a complete disaster. Here's a pick-me-up: Give yourself a treat by making your favorite zucchini sticks. Score one for you!

Makes 4 servings.

Ingredients

½ cup seasoned bread crumbs
2 tablespoons grated
    Parmesan cheese
1 egg
2 small zucchini, cut into
    sticks

Materials

Shallow dish
Spoon (for mixing)
Shallow bowl
Fork, knife
Cookie sheet

1 In a shallow dish, mix together bread crumbs and Parmesan cheese.

2 In a separate bowl, beat egg with a fork.

3 Dip each zucchini stick first in crumb mixture, then in egg. Dip again into crumb mixture until well-coated.

4 Place zucchini sticks on greased cookie sheet (see greasing tip on page 17) and bake at 400 degrees for 15 to 20 minutes, or until browned and crispy.

Tip: Dunk the zucchini sticks in Ranch dip or your favorite salad dressing!

Everyone's Favorite Candied Carrots

You find the coolest stuff out in the alley:
A bamboo pole (makes a great sword).
Discarded trash can lid (shield).
Lamp shade (helmet).
Cardboard refrigerator box (fort).
Now, if you can just get it to your secret hiding place before Mom sees it and makes you put it all back before dinner! "Coming, Mom. I love carrots!"

Makes 3 to 4 servings.

Ingredients

4 carrots, peeled and sliced
1 teaspoon salt
2 tablespoons butter
2 tablespoons brown sugar
1 teaspoon lemon juice

Materials

Knife (for slicing)
Cutting board
Medium saucepan
Large spoon (for stirring)

1 Place sliced carrots in saucepan with enough water to cover; add salt.

2 Cook over high heat until water begins to boil, then reduce heat. Simmer for about 20 minutes, or until carrots are tender.

3 Drain off water and add butter, brown sugar, and lemon juice, stirring until carrots are coated.

Tip: Carrots are a good source of vitamin A, which is important for healthy skin and good vision!

Yummy-in-the-Tummy Macaroni and Cheese

Macaroni and Cheese.
Gotta love it!
It's the number-one favorite food of kids under 12—and over!

Makes 6 servings.

Ingredients

1 pound elbow macaroni,
   cooked and drained
3 tablespoons margarine
1½ cups milk
12 ounces Velveeta cheese,
   grated

Materials

Large saucepan
Large spoon (for stirring)
Casserole dish

1 Preheat oven to 350 degrees.

2 In large saucepan over medium heat, melt margarine and add milk. Stir in cheese and cook until just melted.

3 Gently mix cheese mixture with macaroni and pour into greased (see greasing tip on page 17) casserole dish.

4 Bake at 350 degrees for 15 to 20 minutes, or until bubbly.

Tip: Totally tubular! Or have fun and use different pasta shapes, such as shells, twists, or bow-ties.

Finger-Lickin'-Good Potato Skins

You're going to be an astronaut when you grow up. You'll wear a pressurized suit, defy gravity, and conduct important experiments in space. But do they really have to eat dehydrated food? Maybe you can figure out a way to take along your favorite snack to the moon. After all, they couldn't expect you to last that long without your precious potato skins!

Makes 2 to 4 servings.

Ingredients

2 potatoes
1 tablespoon vegetable oil
4 tablespoons margarine
½ cup cheese, grated
¼ cup sour cream
¼ cup bacon bits
Salt and pepper, to taste

Materials

Fork, knife, spoon
Aluminum foil
Oven-safe dish

1 Preheat oven to 400 degrees

2 Wash potatoes, prick with a fork, and brush skins with oil. Wrap the potatoes in foil and bake at 400 degrees for 1 hour. Cool; then cut in half lengthwise. Cut again lengthwise, to create 4 quarters.

3 Scoop out cooked insides, leaving about ½ inch of cooked potatoes in their skins. (Save the rest of the cooked potatoes for another day.)

4 Arrange the shells in an oven-safe dish and sprinkle shells with salt and pepper. Spread with margarine; then add cheese, sour cream, and bacon bits.

5 Return the shells to the oven to brown for 5 to 10 minutes, until cheese bubbles.

Tip: Add chipped beef or ham to the shells in Step 4, and the skins are a meal in themselves!

Really, Really Good Rice

Company for dinner tonight. You help polish the silver, set the table with the fancy place mats, and then your parents start with the manners review. (Really—you know not to put your elbows on the table.) And what you're really good at is cooking. This rice is everyone's favorite.

Makes 6 servings.

Ingredients

4 cups cooked white or
   brown rice
1 can cream of mushroom
   soup
1 2-ounce can sliced
   mushrooms, drained
½ cup butter or margarine,
   melted

Materials

Casserole dish

1 Preheat oven to 350 degrees.

2 In a greased casserole dish (see greasing tip on page 17), alternate layers of cooked rice, undiluted soup, and mushrooms.

3 Drizzle butter on top and bake at 350 degrees for 20 minutes, or until heated throughout.

Tip: To get 4 cups of cooked rice, you'll have to cook about 1½ to 2 cups raw rice.

Save-the-Best-for-Last Desserts

Ooey-Gooey
Microwave S'Mores

Cooking S'Mores over a campfire can involve:
—getting poked with someone's coat hanger,
—setting your marshmallow on fire, and/or
—dropping your graham cracker in the dirt.
But if you're camping out in the kitchen this weekend, don't worry. Try the microwave.
They're just as good this way (and probably a whole lot safer).

**Makes 1 s'more (double the ingredients for
2 s'mores, triple for 3, and so on).**

Ingredients

2 graham crackers
1 marshmallow, regular
1 square of a chocolate candy
   bar

Materials

Paper towels
Microwave

1 Make a sandwich of 1 marshmallow and a chocolate candy square between 2 graham crackers.

2 Wrap a paper towel around the sandwich and microwave on high for 10 to 20 seconds, or until the chocolate is melted and the marshmallow puffs up.

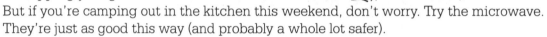

Tip: These can be very hot, so take care not to burn your mouth!

Chocolate Mud Pies with Gummy Worms

It's April Fool's Day, and you have a few tricks up your sleeve. You invite some friends over for chocolate pudding. As you dip your spoon into the creamy confection, you begin to scream with horror. Worms! Worms in the pudding!

Makes 4 servings.

Ingredients

1 4-ounce package instant chocolate pudding
2 cups milk
Gummy Worm candies
½ cup graham cracker crumbs

Materials

Electric mixer
Medium bowl
4 dessert dishes

1 With electric mixer, beat together pudding mix and milk in a bowl for 2 minutes, or until thickened.

2 Pour pudding "mud" into individual dessert dishes and insert gummy worms into pudding.

3 Crush graham crackers and sprinkle graham cracker "dirt" on top of the pudding. Chill.

Tip: Make these pies even more authentic-looking by serving them in miniature clay flower pots (very well washed and lined with aluminum foil!), with a mint sprig "plant" on top.

Easy and Elegant Cherry Surprise

Piano recital tonight. Been practicing for weeks. Got a terrific new dress to wear. Your best friend is coming to hear you, and even if you do flub up a little here and there, she'll still think you're great. (She's like that.) Now…you'll need a great dessert for after the recital. Only the best for your best friend!

Makes 6 to 8 servings.

Ingredients

1 10-ounce can cherry pie filling

1 14-ounce can sweetened condensed milk

1 15-ounce container frozen whipped topping, thawed

1 9-inch graham cracker pie crust

Materials

Large bowl

Large spoon (for mixing)

1 In a bowl, mix together pie filling, condensed milk, and whipped topping.

2 Pour into crust.

3 Freeze pie until serving time.

Tip: To make the pie even more festive, decorate it with maraschino cherries.

Crunchy Cookies-and-Cream Pie

Gin Rummy.
Old Maid.
Go Fish.
Battle.

You win some, you lose some. But the real winner is the so-very-scrumptious treat you've whipped up. What a sweet ending to a fun day!

Makes 6 to 8 servings.

Ingredients

2 dozen chocolate cream-
  filled sandwich cookies
2 tablespoons butter, melted
1 15-ounce container frozen
  whipped topping, thawed
2 pints chocolate ice cream,
  softened

Materials

Plastic bag
Rolling pin
9-inch pie pan
Large bowl

1 Place 12 to 16 cookies in plastic bag and crush with rolling pin.

2 Mix cookie crumbs with melted butter and press into bottom of the pie pan.

3 Separate remaining cookies into halves and stand them up around edge of pie pan, lining the sides. Save remaining cookie halves to decorate top of pie.

4 Combine whipped topping and ice cream in a bowl and spoon into cookie crumb crust. Top with whole cookie halves, or crumble them and sprinkle on top.

5 Cover and freeze for several hours before serving.

Tip: If your pie pan does not have a cover, you can use aluminum foil to cover the pie (so that it doesn't smell like the freezer!).

Spiffy Yogurt Party Parfaits

My Favorite Things:

1. Going to the movies.
2. Talking on the phone with my friends.
3. Long, hot bubble baths.
4. Playing tennis.
5. Oh, and I almost forgot: eating Party Parfaits.

So pretty, you (almost) won't want to eat them!

1 parfait per serving.

Ingredients

Frozen yogurt (any flavor)
Fresh fruit (any kind of berry
   works well)
Frozen whipped topping,
   thawed
Nuts, chopped, or granola

Materials

Tall glass
Spoon

1 Layer small amounts of yogurt and fruit in a tall glass to create colored stripes.

2 Spoon whipped topping on top and add a sprinkle of nuts or granola. Voila—a fancy treat!

Tips: Make as many or as few as you like, depending on the occasion or on your appetite. Experiment with different flavors of frozen yogurt and different fruit, to mix and match colors and flavors.

Melt-in-Your-Mouth Brownies

Roses are red.
Violets are blue.
I l-o-o-v-e chocolate.
How about you?

Makes 2 dozen brownies.

Ingredients

4 squares unsweetened
   chocolate
¾ cup butter or margarine
3 eggs, slightly beaten with
   a fork
2 cups sugar
1 cup flour
½ teaspoon salt
1 teaspoon vanilla

Materials

Large saucepan
Fork, spoon, knife
9-by-13-inch baking pan
Toothpick

1 Preheat oven to 350 degrees.

2 In a large saucepan over low heat, melt chocolate pieces and butter.

3 Remove from heat and stir beaten eggs and sugar into the melted chocolate. Then add flour, salt, and vanilla; mix well.

4 Pour into a greased baking pan (see greasing tip on page 17) and bake at 350 degrees for about 35 minutes, or until inserted toothpick comes out clean.

5 Cool before slicing into squares.

Tip: While melting the chocolate and butter, stir continuously and do not allow the butter to burn—burnt butter has a strong and unpleasant smell.

Yum-Yum-Eat-'Em-Up Gingerbread Men

Run, run,
As fast as you can!
You can't catch me,
I'm the gingerbread man!

Makes about 1 dozen gingerbread men.

Ingredients

⅔ cup butter, softened
½ cup brown sugar
2 teaspoons ginger
1 teaspoon cinnamon
½ teaspoon ground cloves
1 egg
¾ cup molasses
3 cups flour
1 teaspoon baking soda
Raisins
Red hot candies
Tubes of frosting

Materials

Large bowl
Electric mixer
Medium bowl
Sifter
Rolling pin
5-inch gingerbread-man
   cookie cutters
Spatula
Cookie sheet

1 In large mixing bowl, use electric mixer to cream together butter, sugar, spices, egg, and molasses. Blend well.

2 Sift together flour and baking soda in a separate bowl; then add to creamed mixture (see sifting tip on page 30).

3 Preheat oven to 375 degrees.

4 Roll out dough with a rolling pin on a floured surface and cut out shapes with the cookie cutters. Use a spatula to carefully place the cut-out shapes on a lightly greased cookie sheet (see greasing tip on page 17).

5 Use raisins and red hots to make eyes, mouth, and buttons.

6 Bake at 375 degrees for 8 to 10 minutes; then cool. Use tubes of frosting to decorate—belt, hair, and so on.

Tip: You can buy tubes of frosting in the supermarket, in the baking section. The tubes of frosting usually come in different colors, so chose the ones you like.

Classic Chewy Chocolate Chip Cookies

The guys across the street built a tree house and put up a "No Girls Allowed" sign over the entrance. Just sit on the front curb with a plate of freshly-baked chocolate chip cookies, and set your timer. Three minutes.... Oh, hello, boys!

Makes 4 to 5 dozen cookies.

Ingredients

1 cup butter, softened
1 cup sugar
½ cup brown sugar
1 teaspoon vanilla
2 eggs
2¼ cups flour
1 teaspoon baking soda
1 teaspoon salt
2 cups semi-sweet chocolate
    chips

Materials

Large mixing bowl
Electric mixer
Medium bowl
Sifter
Large spoon (for stirring)
Teaspoon
Cookie sheet

1 Preheat oven to 375 degrees.

2 Using electric mixer, beat together butter, sugars, vanilla and eggs in a large bowl.

3 Sift together flour, baking soda, and salt into a separate bowl and mix into egg mixture (see sifting tip on page 30).

4 Stir in chocolate chips and mix well.

5 Drop dough by heaping teaspoonfuls onto ungreased cookie sheet. Bake at 375 degrees for about 10 minutes, or until golden.

Tip: Make the cookies a little larger and use them to build your own ice cream sandwiches!

Ready-to-Decorate Sugar Cookies

For the holidays, you make lots of cookies—angels, stars, and Santas. You can't wait to experiment with those sparkly sugar decorations. After all, everyone's counting on you for your beautiful works of art....It's a tradition!

Makes about 2 dozen cookies.

Ingredients

1 egg
½ cup shortening
2 tablespoons milk
1 cup sugar
1¾ cups flour
2 teaspoons baking powder
½ teaspoon salt
1 teaspoon vanilla

Materials

Large bowl
Electric mixer
Medium bowl
Rolling pin
Cookie cutters
Cookie sheet

1 Preheat oven to 375 degrees.

2 Using electric mixer, cream together egg, shortening, sugar, and milk in a large bowl.

3 Mix together remaining ingredients in a medium bowl and add to egg mixture.

4 Using rolling pin on a floured surface (or waxed paper), roll out dough to about ¼-inch thickness; then cut into shapes with cookie cutters.

5 Place the cookies on a lightly greased cookie sheet (see greasing tip on page 17) and sprinkle shapes with sugar. Bake at 375 degrees for about 8 minutes.

6 Cool before decorating with icing designs or stenciled sugar shapes.

Tip: If you do not have an electric mixer, you can mix by hand, using a fork—but be sure to mix really well.

Fun-to-Make
Peanut Butter Cookies

Your first dance, and Sarabeth didn't seem to notice that you stepped on her new black party shoes. Then you escorted her to the refreshment table, and she mentioned that she had made the cookies. They were delicious....I think I'm in love!

Makes about 3 dozen cookies.

Ingredients

1 cup butter
1 cup sugar
1 cup brown sugar
1 cup peanut butter
2 eggs
2¼ cups flour
2 teaspoons soda
¼ teaspoon salt
1 teaspoon vanilla

Materials

Large bowl
Electric mixer
Medium bowl
Sifter
Rolling pin
Fork
Cookie sheet

1 Preheat oven to 350 degrees.

2 With electric mixer, beat together butter, white and brown sugars, and peanut butter in a large bowl.

3 Add eggs and beat with the rest of the butter mixture.

4 In a medium bowl, sift together flour, soda, and salt (see sifting tip on page 30); then add to egg mixture. Add in vanilla.

5 Roll the dough into balls on a floured surface and flatten with a fork, making a criss-cross design. (Dipping fork in ice water will prevent it from sticking to the dough.)

6 Bake on greased cookie sheet at 350 degrees for 8 minutes (see greasing tip on page 17).

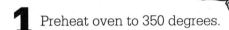

Tip: Substitute a 10-ounce bag of peanut butter chips for the peanut butter. Tastes great!

Grandma's Best Oatmeal Cookies

Your grandma lets you help her bake. You get to measure, stir—and lick the spoon! She doesn't even care when you spill flour all over the floor, because you're cooking up a great batch of cookies…and some wonderful memories!

Makes about 3 dozen cookies.

Ingredients

1 cup shortening
1 cup sugar
1 cup brown sugar
2 eggs
1 teaspoon vanilla
2 cups flour
1 teaspoon baking soda
1 teaspoon salt
3 cups quick-cooking oats
1 cup raisins

Materials

Large bowl
Electric mixer
Medium bowl
Large spoon, teaspoon
Cookie sheet

1 Preheat oven to 350 degrees.

2 With electric mixer, cream together shortening, white and brown sugars, eggs, and vanilla in a large bowl.

3 In a medium bowl sift together flour, salt, and soda and add to egg mixture (see sifting tip on page 30). Fold in oatmeal with a large spoon.

4 Drop dough by teaspoonful onto cookie sheet and bake at 350 degrees for 10 to 12 minutes.

5 Cool before serving.

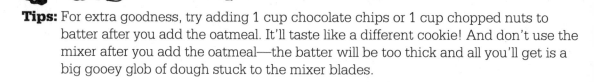

Tips: For extra goodness, try adding 1 cup chocolate chips or 1 cup chopped nuts to batter after you add the oatmeal. It'll taste like a different cookie! And don't use the mixer after you add the oatmeal—the batter will be too thick and all you'll get is a big gooey glob of dough stuck to the mixer blades.

Index

INDEX

INDEX

G

Gelatin
   cups, 63
   shapes, 41
Gingerbread men, 92
Granola, 34
Grape juice drink, 5
Grilled cheese sandwich, 52

H

Ham and cheese rollups, 55
Hamburgers 75
Hash browns, 21

J

Juice bars, frozen, 43

L

Lemonade, 6

M

Macaroni and cheese, 81
Meat loaves, mini, 71
Melon boats, 62
Mud pies, 87
Muffins
   banana, 29
   corn, 31
   strawberry, 30

N

Nachos and salsa, 45

O

Oatmeal, 18
Oatmeal drops, no-bake, 37
Oatmeal cookies, 96

Omelets, cheese, 16
Orange fizz, 7

P

Pancakes, blueberry, 13
Peach cooler, 10
Peanut butter cookies, 95
Pie
   cherry, 88
   chocolate mud, 87
   cookies and cream, 89
Pigs in the blanket, 49
Pizza, 48
Popcorn, caramel, 38
Popovers, 24
Pops, banana, 42
Potato
   hash browns, 21
   skins, 82
   soup, 58
Purple drink, 5

Q

Quesadillas, bean and cheese, 56

R

Raisin bagels, 32
Rice, mushroom, 83
Rolls, cinnamon, 26
Root beer float, 9

S

Salad
   carrot and raisin, 61
   taco, 65
   tossed green, 64
   tuna, 50, 66

INDEX

Kids' Party Cookbook

by Penny Warner
Illustrated by Laurel Aiello

Over 175 reduced-fat recipes are included in this book—recipes that are fun and tasty for kids, but full of nutrition to please parents. Warner has fun ideas for every meal, including mini-meals, such as Peanut Butter Burger Dogs and Twinkle Sandwiches; creative snacks, such as Aquarium Jell-O and Prehistoric Bugs; creative desserts, such as Spaghetti Ice Cream; and holiday fare, such as Jack O' Lantern Custard for Halloween. (Ages 8 and up)

Order #2435 $12.00

Kids' Holiday Fun

by Penny Warner
Illustrated by Kathy Rogers

Penny Warner's book gives you fun ideas for entertaining your children during 34 different holidays, including New Year's, Valentine's Day, St. Patrick's Day, Fourth of July, Halloween, and Christmas. Every single month of the year, your family can turn to this comprehensive guide for delicious holiday recipes, decoration suggestions, instructions for fun holiday activities and games, party ideas, and crafts.

Order #6000 $12.00

Kids' Party Games and Activities

by Penny Warner
Illustrated by Kathy Rogers

This is the most complete guide to party games and activities for kids aged 2–12! It contains illustrated descriptions, instructions, rules, and trouble-shooting tips for 300 games and activities (more than triple the number in other books), including traditional and contemporary games, simple and elaborate activities, plus ideas for outings, events, and entertainers.

Order #6095 $12.00

The Best Birthday Party Game Book

by Bruce Lansky

This unique birthday party book contains eight entertaining games and activities that get everyone involved in the festivities. Complete with tear-out duplicate game sheets for party guests, this book will "break the ice" and get the celebration off to a fast and funny start.

Order #6064 $3.95

Poetry Party

by Bruce Lansky
Illustrated by Stephen Carpenter

The "King of Giggle Poetry" has put together an all-new collection that has more laugh-out-loud poems than any other children's poetry book. Lansky had the help of more than 1,000 elementary-school students and their teachers in choosing the funniest poems about such subjects as parents who won't let their kids watch TV, yucky school lunches, and dogs that "water" the flowers. (Ages 6-12)

"Bruce Lansky is the Pied Piper of Poetry."

— "Dear Teacher" nationally syndicated columnist,
Marge Eberts

Order #2430 $12.00 hardcover

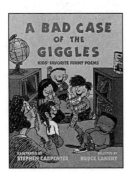

A Bad Case of the Giggles

Selected by Bruce Lansky
Illustrated by Stephen Carpenter

Bruce Lansky knows that a book that makes children laugh helps motivate them to read more often. That's why this book will turn your kids into poetry lovers. Every poem included in this book had to pass the giggle test of over 600 school children. This anthology collects the royal court of children's poets (court jesters all): Shel Silverstein, Jack Prelutsky, Judith Viorst, Jeff Moss, and Lansky himself.

The American Booksellers Association has chosen this book as "Pick of the Lists" for children's poetry.

Order #2411 $15.00 hardcover

Kids Pick the Funniest Poems

Compiled by Bruce Lansky
Illustrated by Stephen Carpenter

Three hundred elementary-school kids will tell you that this book contains the funniest poems for kids—because they picked them! Not surprisingly, they chose many of the funniest poems ever written by favorites like Shel Silverstein, Jack Prelutsky, Jeff Moss, and Judith Viorst (plus poems by lesser known writers that are just as funny). This book is guaranteed to please children ages 6–12!

Order #2410 $15.00 hardcover

Girls to the Rescue

Edited by Bruce Lansky

This collection of ten folk and fairy tales featuring courageous, clever, and determined girls from around the world is the first in the *Girls to the Rescue* series. This groundbreaking book will update traditional fairy tales for girls ages 8–12.

"Girls to the Rescue turns a new page and Prince Charming is history."

—Sally Han, *New York Daily News*

Order #2215 $3.95

Girls to the Rescue, Book #2

Edited by Bruce Lansky

Here is the second groundbreaking collection of folk tales featuring ten clever and courageous girls from around the world. Among the heroes in this book you will meet Jamila, a girl who saves her village from a terrible tiger; Adrianna, a Mexican girl who rescues her family's farm from ruin; and Vassilisa, a Russian aristocrat who saves her brother from prison. (Ages 8-12)

"Girls to the Rescue strongly affirms the character of young girls, encouraging them to rely on their own uniqe strengths and talents."

—Jennifer Stevenson, *St. Petersburg Times*

Order #2217 $12.00 hardcover
Order #2216 $3.95 paperback

Girls to the Rescue, Book #3

Edited by Bruce Lansky

The runaway success of the *Girls to the Rescue* series continues with this third collection of folk tales from around the world, featuring such heroic girls as Emily, a girl who helps a runaway slave and her baby daughter reach safety and freedom; Sarah, a Polish girl who saves her father from prison; and Kamala, a Punjabi girl who outsmarts a pack of thieves. (Ages 8-12)

" Inspiring."

—Mary Hance, *Nashville Banner*

Order #2219 $3.95

Available April '97

Order Form

Qty.	Title	Author	Order No.	Unit Cost (U.S. $)	Total
	Bad Case of the Giggles	Lansky, B.	2411	$15.00	
	Best Birthday Party Game Book	Lansky, B.	6064	$3.95	
	Dads Say the Dumbest Things!	Lansky/Jones	4220	$6.00	
	Free Stuff for Kids	Free Stuff Editors	2190	$5.00	
	Girls to the Rescue	Lansky, B.	2215	$3.95	
	Girls to the Rescue, Book #2	Lansky, B.	2216	$3.95	
	Girls to the Rescue, Book #3	Lansky, B.	2219	$3.95	
	Kids Are Cookin'	Brown, K.	2440	$8.00	
	Kids' Holiday Fun	Warner, P.	6000	$12.00	
	Kids' Party Cookbook	Warner, P.	2435	$12.00	
	Kids' Party Games and Activities	Warner, P.	6095	$12.00	
	Kids Pick the Funniest Poems	Lansky, B.	2410	$15.00	
	Moms Say the Funniest Things!	Lansky, B.	4280	$6.00	
	New Adventures of Mother Goose	Lansky, B.	2420	$15.00	
	Poetry Party	Lansky, B.	2430	$12.00	
				Subtotal	
			Shipping and Handling (see below)		
			MN residents add 6.5% sales tax		
				Total	

YES! Please send me the books indicated above. Add $2.00 shipping and handling for the first book and 50¢ for each additional book. Add $2.50 to total for books shipped to Canada. Overseas postage will be billed. Allow up to four weeks for delivery. Send check or money order payable to Meadowbrook Press. No cash or COD's, please. Prices subject to change without notice. **Quantity discounts available upon request.**

Send book(s) to:

Name _____ Address_____

City _____ State _____ Zip _____

Telephone (_____)_____ P.O. number (if necessary) _____

Payment via:

❑ Check or money order payable to Meadowbrook Press (No cash or COD's, please)   Amount enclosed $ _____

❑ Visa (for orders over $10.00 only) ❑ MasterCard (for orders over $10.00 only)

Account # _____ Signature _____ Exp. Date _____

A _FREE_ Meadowbrook Press catalog is available upon request.

You can also phone us for orders of $10.00 or more at 1-800-338-2232.

Mail to: **Meadowbrook Press**

5451 Smetana Drive, Minnetonka, MN 55343

Phone (612) 930-1100   Toll-Free 1-800-338-2232   Fax (612) 930-1940